Sales

Evolution

Cultural Vision

for Strategic Leaders

Also by Bill Sinunu

Evolving Globe Series:

Business —

HR Evolution
Student Evolution
Asian Student Evolution

Travel —

Living Without Borders

Details at BillSinunu.com.

About Bill Sinunu

BILL SINUNU, MA, a University of Chicago-trained Master Facilitator and author of two best-selling books, is a cross-cultural speaker, trainer and consultant. In the Evolving Globe Series, look for business books *HR Evolution, Student Evolution* and coming soon, *Asian Student Evolution*.

Additionally, he is a Ted Talk presenter and board member at Purdue University's Center for International Business Education and Research. The former airline executive offers culturally insightful keynotes, training and coaching for his corporate and university clients.

Sinunu, who is tri-lingual, is a former interpreter for the US Department of Immigration/Customs and was appointed to a U.S. Department of Health and Human Services task force.

Praise for Bill Sinunu

"Bill invites you to participate in his worldly travels and consider the scope of a wildly diverse planet."

Greg Kinnear
Actor, Academy Award nominee and Sinunu fan

"Sinunu traverses cultures and individuals— and the outcome is a mosaic of thoughts and feelings that is at once both universal and personal. A rare feat."

Tal Ben-Shahar, PhD
Professor – Harvard University

Sales Evolution

*Cultural Vision
for Strategic Leaders*

First Edition

By Bill Sinunu M.A.

William Sinunu, 2013, Publisher

Table of Contents

Introduction

The writing is on the wall. If US corporations plan to maintain a leadership role in the global marketplace, employees have to acquire a global perspective. For years, American executives have questioned the return on investment for soft skill education and, in particular, scoffed at the idea of cross-cultural training. However, as our business world becomes increasingly interactive and internationally focused, culturally sensitive approaches are essential for professional and respectful communication.

Beyond raising corporate reputations to a more sophisticated level, cross-cultural education maintains profitable relationships. As many in global entities already know, one inappropriate email, comment or interaction can easily damage or even ruin an international relationship. Basic cultural education, such as the significance of color selection when sending a package to Tokyo, understanding email verbiage from Mumbai, how to properly return a banquet toast in Shanghai or understanding business norms in Cairo not only cultivates and strengthens relationships, but it eliminates costly misunderstandings.

Strengthen your Market Position and Prepare your Company for the Future

As global mergers, alliances and agreements become common practice, the need for cross-cultural knowledge will become increasingly important at all levels. But the clock is ticking and the likelihood that executives may have to learn cross-cultural awareness under extenuating circumstances is a growing concern.

For example, stories abound regarding Detroit-based Chrysler executives who struggled in Daimler's corporate culture. Not only were seasoned American executives surrounded by another language, leaders were stunned by German corporate norms and many floundered in the new environment. It's hard enough to adjust to a new corporate culture during a domestic merger, but when a partner is from another country, an entire new set of obstacles quickly becomes evident. It takes specific training and education for individuals, departments and organizations to progress down the cultural learning curve.

Global Education Increases Service Levels, Builds Stronger Teams and Maximizes Revenue Potential.

Companies who set aside ethnocentric tendencies and better connect with international partners and foreign investors will flourish and succeed. Managers who fully understand a range of cultural behaviors—from Japanese negotiation techniques and Chinese superstitions to Middle Eastern norms and South American communication style—will become the visionary leaders of tomorrow. Additionally, future leaders will get a leg up on their competition by including outsourced workers (who often provide customer service and reservations functions) into cultural trainings and global networks. Certainly all organizations can benefit from higher service levels, stronger teams, increased revenues and a more inclusive corporate culture.

Standardizing Best Practices across Corporate Divisions Improves Quality Control, Streamlines Operations, Enhances Customer Service and Creates a Unified Corporate Culture.

Another key to global success: organizations with international sites should solicit and value input from *all* employees in *all* divisions. Although creating and facilitating international focus groups sounds like a simple task, the endeavor contains inherent challenges, including conflicting cross-cultural communication styles, differing cultural attitudes towards hierarchies, navigating levels of fluency and methods to overcome cultural norms that inhibit communication.

The time is now to raise the bar for global business. The formula for success is simple: comprehensive cross-cultural education that will evolve your organization and move players down the cross-cultural knowledge curve. Get on board. This book will show you the way. It's one of the best investments you can make to position yourself and your company for an increasingly interactive global marketplace.

Understanding the Terminology Enhances the Global Education Experience.

For the sake of clarity, c*ultural awareness* and *cultural competence* are phrases comprising keystone terminology associated with evolving and increasing one's overall comprehension of any given culture—either through an individual, corporate or academic lens.

Cultural knowledge of any given culture's characteristics, idiosyncrasies and mores, along with an overall *awareness* of differing cultural values and expectations lead to *cultural competence*. *Cultural intelligence* also includes other layers of awareness and practice, which will be discussed as we go along. By the time you finish this book, you will be well on your way to *cultural competence.*

Throughout this book the reader will notice various points where these terms and other similar terminology are emphasized via italics and/or bold. The intent is to draw attention to the importance of their concepts and implementation within organizations.

Chapter 1

Going Global

So many companies have "gone global" but I can't help but wonder if it's just a label. Certainly, there may be worldwide divisions and often, a "global" headquarters. But how many of these departments or companies are led by savvy global leaders or staffed by culturally knowledgeable employees?

Moving the needle and initiating a *cultural transformation* starts with you. Ask yourself the five following questions and think about how you can enhance not only your worldwide vision, but how you can alter your behavior and/or actions to fit the global leader role.

1. *Do I have a thirst for knowledge and am I open to self-improvement?* Global leaders are driven and known to be the best in their field. If you are on a path to learn as much as you can about your area of expertise, then you are on the right track.

2. *Am I responsible and have I paved my own path*? Research shows global leaders have a history of being accountable and resourceful from a young age. For example, did you work from a young age? Pay for your own education? How responsible are you for your success?

3. *Am I ethical and do I believe in hard work*? Global leaders possess a high level of integrity, honesty, respect for time and social responsibility. If you haven't always taken the high road, now is the time to start.

4. *Am I well educated and embracing my academic training*? Global leaders have strong analytical skills and are creative in their thought process. They are active

in extracurricular activities that have developed their social, team and leadership skill set. Immerse yourself in leadership education and get everything you can out of it.

5. *Am I open to learning from others* in a variety of venues—individuals, cultures, and role models? Find balance—in addition to your professional endeavors, explore extracurricular activities that interest you. Much of your social and cross-cultural knowledge can be gleaned through social groups.

Chapter 2

Moving Down the Path

Hopefully you found the first exercise thought provoking and helpful. Now let's move on to the next building block. To become a world citizen, you need to be adept both *globally* and *culturally*. *Global knowledge* relates to hard facts and *cultural knowledge* relates to people—in particular—cultural norms, values, mores, ways of communicating and traditions. Let's start with the hard facts. The following exercise will establish a foundation of global knowledge.

To gain credibility, you have to walk the talk and lead by example. If you are truly enthusiastic about being a global player, you have to know your stuff. Follow the simple four-week plan below and you will be off to a great start and on the path to enhancing your current level of global knowledge. All of the information is easily accessible on your computer.

Week 1 — Memorize World Capitals

Get your flash cards ready and you can knock this out. As Americans, we memorized all 50 state capitals in elementary school. Now it's time to expand our vision. Take a different continent every day and simply memorize every world capital on that continent. It will take about an hour a day— think of it as homework.

Week 2 — Memorize World Languages

This module may seem easy and for many countries, it is. Germans speak German, Japanese speak Japanese and Greeks speak Greek. However, there are several exceptions. For example, in Singapore, there are four official languages—English, Malay, Mandarin and Tamil. Once again, get your flashcards ready and conquer a different continent every day.

Hang in there—you are almost there.

Week 3 — Memorize World Religions

Now we are on to world religions. Approach this week differently than earlier modules. Take the primary world religions and list them—Christianity, Judaism, Muslim, Buddhism, and so on. Then list the countries by primary religion underneath the heading and memorize the list accordingly. For example, although Canadians represent a number of religious denominations, the primary religion is Christianity. Keep it simple. You can learn secondary religions later. This module will provide a framework for you to build upon.

Week 4 — Memorize World Currencies

Take a different continent every day and prepare your flashcards. Many countries have had the same currency for decades while others are in the process of transition or have already transitioned. A prime example is the evolution of the euro, but don't assume all European countries have transitioned to the euro. Countries like Germany, Italy and France have all adopted the euro, but there are several notables like the United Kingdom and Denmark who have retained the pound and krone, respectively.

Week 5 (optional) — World Airports, Airline Alliances

In my social experience with international executives (dinner conversations, etc.), conversation invariably gravitates to travel schedules, past and future business trips, favorite airlines/ hotel chains, and so on. It's a "safe" topic and one that global players typically can all embrace. In order to interact as a savvy traveler, it is helpful if you know major airports (Tokyo—Narita, London—Heathrow, etc.) and individual airlines in alliances (Star, OneWorld, etc.). In addition, for many hierarchically sensitive cultures (we will cover this in depth later.), the hotels you frequent, business/ first class airline travel, and such, are vitally important in how you are perceived and your level of influence. Get your flashcards out; one more week... you can do it.

Chapter 3

Getting Onboard

Now that you have a solid individual foundation as a global leader, it's time to start relaying your knowledge and enthusiasm to your team. Implement the following global enhancements to your department to initiate an awareness and culture swing.

1. Walk The Talk

It all starts at the top. In meetings with your team, enthusiastically outline what you have accomplished and share your global vision. Discuss the four-week plan with your cohort and encourage them to hop on board by familiarizing themselves with the world's capitals, languages, religions and currencies.

2. Weekly Tips

As your department becomes familiar with the four modules listed above, send out weekly tips. Start a "Did You Know...." communication via poster board, update in meetings or a fun multiple choice quiz email. For example, "Did You Know the following European countries all use the euro—Germany, Greece, Italy, Ireland and several European countries do not , including United Kingdom (British pound), Denmark (krone), Hungary (forint) and Iceland (krone)?" It's at this juncture you can start introducing cultural material. Everybody can learn together.

More examples:

-- *"Did you know French high school students must pass a Philosophy exam in order to graduate?" (Recognizing that philosophy is important to the culture provides insight into French social priorities i.e. self-reflection, arts, and so forth. Knowing these bits of information can help sales executives initiate conversations around topics that will build cross-cultural bonds.).*

-- *"Did you know showing the heels of your shoes to another in the Middle East is considered disrespectful and rude?"* (Be careful crossing your legs at the ankle when hosting an executive from the Middle East or visiting cities like Cairo or Dubai.)

-- *"Why was August 8, 2008 one of the most profitable days in history for florists in San Francisco?"* (San Francisco has a large Chinese population who are linked to their heritage. In China, 8 is considered a lucky number so on 8/8/08, thousands of red roses (according to Chinese lore, red brings good fortune) were sent across the city to friends and family.).

3. Make Quality Circles into Communication Circles

All good managers meet regularly with their staff and ask a variety of questions, such as "How can I better support you? Do you have the tools to do your job properly?" I suggest you add another question to your interactions: "Are you confused or frustrated by your interactions with clients or peers from other cultures?" I guarantee you will be amazed by the response. For example, many front line service employees are baffled by the behavior of Indian clients. However, by educating employees about the Indian caste culture, front line employees will be better equipped to effectively interact and understand how they are perceived in their service role (more details on the caste system to follow). You can lead the way and enlighten your employees by educating yourself about cross-cultural communication styles, e.g. direct vs. indirect communicators, how to overcome the four primary obstacles to cross cultural communication and the importance of embracing *cultural empathy*. I will cover this in depth shortly—read on.

4. International Holidays and Events

Embrace diversity. Cater a monthly luncheon with a different cultural fare every month. Celebrate holidays by tapping into your resources. For example, invite your Muslim employees to help you and your employees understand and celebrate Ramadan or invite your Jewish employees to share Passover festivities. Open up the celebrations to suppliers and clients too—it sends a wonderful message.

5. Ongoing Education

The journey is ongoing—there is not only much to learn but values and traditions are fluid and often change or alter. Develop an in-house education center or contract a cross-cultural education firm to keep your knowledge base fresh and current.

Chapter 4
Overcoming Obstacles

There are four main obstacles to functional communication between cultures.

> ➤ Varying Cross-Cultural Communication Styles
> ➤ Levels of Fluency
> ➤ Perceptions of Hierarchy
> ➤ Conflicting Norms for Decision Making

Although this section may appear intensely academic, I will provide a variety of examples to illustrate the main points.

Cross-Cultural Communication Styles

There are two types of communicators: *Direct* and *Indirect* communicators.

Direct communicators tend to be verbal, transparent, forthright and assertive (American, German, and Russian).

Indirect communicators tend to be non-verbal, passive and contemplative (Japanese, Taiwanese, and Chinese).

If we lined up all the cultures in the world, the cultures listed above would occupy the extreme positions on the cultural spectrum. Although the rest of the world's cultures would be between them, they tend to fall on one side or the other in the spectrum.

Other examples of *Direct Communicating Cultures* include Scandinavian, Israeli, British, Canadian, and Australian.

Other examples of *Indirect Communicating Cultures* include Indian, Middle Eastern, Central/South American and North/Central African.

Understanding communication styles is vital to working with individuals who have a different background than your own. I recall having breakfast in a hotel in Indianapolis. Adjacent to me were two gentlemen, wearing suits. One was American and the other was Turkish. The American was assertive, forthright and his voice carried throughout the restaurant. He was bent forward in an aggressive position as he delivered his sales pitch. He talked very quickly as sweat broke out on his brow and he hardly took a breath. Meanwhile, the Turkish executive sat back in his chair and listened with little reaction. On occasion, he sipped his coffee, but said not a word. Based on the conversation, this was clearly a business deal the American wanted to quickly solidify. As the American stood, he said, "I have laid out the plan, let's go back up to the suite and sign the paperwork." The Turkish man remained seated and silently sipped on his orange juice. After about a minute, the American awkwardly sat back down and began to babble even faster and louder—once again reiterating his pitch. The reality—the American executive was derailed and he began to panic as evidenced by his heightened hand motions and booming voice. Unlike many indirect communicating cultures, Americans are typically not comfortable with silence. However, the Turkish gentleman, in his non-verbal and non-confrontational style, indicated he was not willing to be "railroaded" into making a deal. In typical indirect communicating style, the Turkish executive wanted to digest the material and sat silently as he pondered. As the American escalated, the Turkish gentleman crossed his arms and shrunk back in his chair, his body language and facial expression indicating his displeasure.

Self-perception is the key. What many Americans don't realize is that many indirect communicators, especially those who hail from small, third world cultures (many of which are collective cultures) are leery and suspect of fast-paced individualistic Americans who have a reputation for being self-serving.

Cultures are deemed either direct or indirect because of generalizations based on cultural norms and values. However there are, as always, exceptions to the rule as noted in the following.

Although Indians are typically indirect

communicators, they can shift (as a product of a caste-oriented society) and become very verbal and sometimes even confrontational if they feel they are addressing someone who they perceive is from an inferior social class.

Another example may be those who hail from indirect communicating cultures, but have been educated in the US or England (and there are many Middle Easterners, Asians, etc. who have been down this path) who have become more direct and western in their communications as a result of their newfound environments and experiences.

Or perhaps those you encounter may have a last name that indicates they are from an indirect communicating culture i.e. Singh, Chang, and Yamaguchi but are actually a product of a blended family—one parent is from a direct communicating culture and the other from an indirect communicating culture.

And finally, sometimes the cultural shoe just doesn't fit. I was facilitating an MBA orientation and encountered a Chinese student who was very outspoken and a major player in classroom exercises. He later told me although he is Chinese, he always felt his behavior was different than his peers and he became even more western in his interaction style after being a tour guide for foreigners during the Olympics in Beijing.

Yet, another factor may be generational. For example, an American peer who is first generation Japanese may communicate indirectly whereas a fourth generation Japanese peer may possess a very direct and typically American style.

The more familiar you become with communication styles and, in particular, the attributes of communication styles different from your own, the more your level of *cultural empathy* will increase. **Cultural empathy** refers to understanding the challenges and mindset of cultures different from your own. Adapting a culturally empathic mindset will allow you to not only understand another cultural style, but more effectively interact and relate to social situations that otherwise may be baffling to you. As you become more culturally astute and empathic, a *culturally competent* "citizen of the world," you will see that your **ethnocentric** (judging another culture based on the values of your culture) tendencies dissipate.

Here is an example of cultural empathy at work: If you, as an American, are working on a multicultural group project, you may be mystified and frustrated by the lack of group cohesion and the inability of the group to move forward. For example, although a Japanese participant is very present— constantly assessing group dynamics and body language—initially he (and I say "he" because Japanese delegations are typically led by males) is typically silent. Americans often perceive Asian silence in groups as passive-aggressive or even hostile behavior. On the flip side, it's important for Americans to understand other player's cultural norms. An American's "take charge and organize the group" actions are often perceived by indirect communicators (in this case, the Japanese participant) as overtly aggressive and dominating.

Let's look at the dynamics. Americans, as citizens raised in a society where "all men are created equal," often feel comfortable expressing their opinion. In addition, Americans often equate strong leadership style with high productivity. However, the Japanese see quality leadership differently. From the Japanese perspective, a slow methodical process holds more importance than productivity as the main path to success. The Japanese have to establish trust and a relationship before expressing their opinion and engaging with a potential business partner. Additionally, Japanese executives feel they need to intuitively understand the players in the group. Furthermore, the Japanese culture does not have the "we are equal" approach and members who are seen as having the most experience and social status are the first individuals to initiate a dialogue. In addition, both cultures are ethnocentric (as most cultures are) and tend to see their approach as superior. The result: a "stand-off" and lack of group cohesion and progress.

In Japan, strategies or decisions on how to proceed with a challenge often take great amounts of time and a thorough examination of the repercussions of each decision. However, in American business, the priority is to keep moving and forge ahead. The American cultural norm is forgiving if one makes a mistake. In fact, American leaders love innovation and often encourage their team to take risks. "We tried that and it didn't work. Let's try another approach." is not an uncommon attitude. However, in Japan, the Japanese look at every decision from all angles before moving ahead. As a result, Americans typically see Japanese business as excruciatingly slow while Japanese often see Americans as "loose cannons" making strategic decisions carelessly.

Interestingly, it is not merely a few select Asian cultures who perceive American leaders as overly hasty and quick to make decisions. Many German executives consider the American decision-making style as overly focused on productivity with too little emphasis on following a logical, strategic process and quality decision making. By German standards, America's business obsession with experimentation is often considered too risky. In contrast, many American executives see the German decision-making style as too detailed, laborious and cautious. In an American company, the executive responsible for a portion of a project is expected to know his or her segment of the project inside and out—but anything outside of their department is typically not considered his or her domain. In general, in America, other portions of a project are left to executives in their respective departments. However, in a German company, every senior executive expects to be briefed and is expected to be up to speed about every aspect of the project—not just what is transpiring within their own department. In addition, when leaders convene, it would not be surprising for each executive to question and directly ask other executives detailed questions about their segment of the operation. In other words, each German executive often takes on the role of a project leader for the entire endeavor. Yet, in the US, if an executive were to question another executive (of similar rank, from another department) in detail about their segment of the project, it would be perceived as hostile, aggressive and inappropriate behavior. In the US, executives tend to be territorial in regard to their departments and take on a "mind your own business" reaction or "you take care of your department, I'll take care of mine" attitude if and/or when a peer questions them.

These are just a few examples of different cultural approaches to business—and there are many—but once you understand the mindset of different cultures and their corresponding norms and values, you can strategize your role accordingly.

Levels of Fluency

It may be on a subconscious level, but we often make judgments about intelligence, capabilities, and other attributes based on an individual's level of fluency. I can't begin to tell you the number of times I have facilitated cross-cultural focus groups and a brilliant participant has been dismissed or ignored because of their inability to verbalize their input clearly in the host language. Americans are at a distinct advantage because many meetings are conducted in English. But, once again, it's important for English speakers to put their "cultural empathy hat" on in a multicultural environment and speak slowly (without coming across in a patronizing manner), ask open-ended questions, and avoid overly technical words. Also, ask questions to clarify: "Ling, when you said _____, what did you mean?"

In general, I find the whole notion of fluency to be very subjective. Are any of us ever really fluent in a second language? Learning a different language is an ongoing process for everyone. It's sometimes impossible to determine a point at which we can say our vocabulary has evolved enough to be able to claim fluency. I find myself discovering new words in English on an ongoing basis, yet I consider myself fluent in my language of origin.

In spite of years of experience and practice with more than one language, I can personally relate to having the fluency rug pulled out from underneath me. A few years ago I was contracted to do some short-term consulting work with a French company. During the interview, which was conducted in English by a non-French speaking interviewer, I confirmed my knowledge of French. However, I was lost during project meetings and had to eventually excuse myself from the gig. My knowledge of French is purely conversational and when it came to French business words (like "leverage" and "strategy" or business terms like "data sets," "marketing profiles" and "business plans"), I found myself only understanding bits and pieces of the dialogue. It was at that point that I wondered—how do we define fluency?

My personal opinion about fluency and how to define the term is best summed up in this way: we are fluent in a language when we can think in that language. Up until that point of seamless transition within our brain, we tend to think about a phrase or word in our native language and then we make the translation leap. As we become more fluent, the translation time decreases. Then there is that magic moment where one is completely immersed, comfortable and present in the communication and interaction process. I believe that is fluency.

I often find international employees of American companies saying over and over again, "I am so sorry for my English." My response, which typically elicits a smile, is "Your English is so much better than my Mandarin. I am delighted you are here and you are an important addition to the team."

Do everything you can to make all

participants feel comfortable and understood. It will come back to you and your organization many times over.

Perceptions of Hierarchy

Many Americans don't recognize how social strata and gender often affect intercultural dynamics. As mentioned earlier, the Indian culture is very caste sensitive; but many other cultures—mainly indirect communicating cultures—are also affected by hierarchical perceptions.

As mentioned earlier, one of America's values, "All Men Are Created Equal," creates an environment where Americans feel comfortable voicing their opinion. Certainly there are some filters. For example, Americans may be aware of their status in a company such that a manager may be reluctant to publicly disagree with a vice-president's decision. In spite of such scenarios, Americans generally feel comfortable expressing their opinion. In fact, many American middle managers feel compelled to speak out when in the midst of senior executives. The mid-level players view the opportunity as a chance to impress the senior executives. However, in more docile and laid back indirect communicating business cultures, members tend to take a more passive position, assess the players and selectively participate.

Another example regarding different perceptions of hierarchy is found in Japan where the oldest and most experienced member of a team will typically be the first to voice his opinion and set the tone. The reason for this is simple—as far as the Japanese culture is concerned: it would be considered disrespectful for a more junior person to disagree with a seasoned, senior member. And that attitude and sense of respecting elders and experience in the field permeates much of Asia.

Hierarchy affects many industries within each culture. Several years ago a Korean airliner, preparing to land, was far short of the runway. In addition, even though the First Officer knew they were on a path to disaster, he was reluctant to express his opinion and question the older and more experienced Captain's lead. A questioning subordinate would be considered disrespectful and cause the Captain to lose "face." The First Officer remained silent as the plane catapulted into the English countryside, several miles short of the runway.

Gender also plays a dominant role in cultural communication. In many indirect communicating cultures, women are not permitted to play a visionary role. Men typically dominate upper management and women often carry out the instructions. I have seen this time and time again in Asia. Women—typically only one, maybe two at the most—sit in silence in a group meeting. The men discuss strategy and when a decision has been reached, one of the men turns to the sole female member and assigns her to carry out the task. Although there are indications this may be changing, currently it's simply the cultural business norm in much of Asia.

A good friend of mine is a very accomplished Japanese woman who lives in the US. She has been in New York for over thirty years and has built a solid and profitable cosmetics company. When we interact, she is very American in her behavior—assertive, outspoken and demanding. However, I had the opportunity to see her in action while interacting with Japanese executives and her demeanor was completely different. She was demure, soft spoken and deferential. She used her charm and language abilities to build trust and close the deal with Japanese associates. Of course she is at a distinct advantage with her Japanese clients because of her appearance and language abilities. Nonetheless, she uses her **cultural chameleon** skill set (We'll talk more about this.) and adapts her personality to accomplish her business goals.

It's also important to be aware of certain political situations and world history. These dynamics can also play a role in hierarchical perception. Several years ago, I was facilitating a seminar for Asian executives. The title of the seminar was "Understanding American Business," and naturally, I included a module on contrasting communication styles. Within the group, there were two large contingents of Chinese and Taiwanese executives. I made the mistake of presenting both cultures in the same sentence—"Chinese and Taiwanese cultures have the same indirect communication style."

I immediately sensed the entire group stiffen and disengage. Members of the group had misunderstood my analogy and thought I was inferring the Chinese and Taiwanese were the same people. Quickly I called a break and although I was aware of the political tensions between China and Taiwan, I didn't realize putting them under the same communication style umbrella would cause such havoc. A Chinese participant discreetly told me during a break, "We are nothing like the Taiwanese. They are lazy and think they are better than others." A Taiwanese participant who overheard the comment quickly added, "The Chinese are loud and have no manners." I quickly had to go into damage control by separating and consoling both the Taiwanese and Chinese participant. Directly after the break, I addressed the issue with the group and explained my comment. It took some time but we got back on track.

Conflicting Norms for Decision Making

When Americans congregate as a team and approach a challenge, the cultural norm prevails. Most American members, regardless of social status, gender, race, etc., typically feel they have the "green light" to participate. However, that is not the case in many other cultures as the previous examples have illustrated. In addition to cultural norms and perceptions of hierarchy, there are often differing norms for reaching strategic decisions.

A classic example in the industry is a case study of an American company operating in Korea. An American multicultural company had a problem. The company plant, just outside of Seoul, was way below output goals and the VP in the US, after a number of conference calls, was not able to get to the bottom of it. The Korean team had been vague in their description of the glitch and the VP decided to send one of his most capable staff members, an operations specialist, to take care of the problem. The woman he decided to deploy to Seoul was a tall, strapping redhead with over thirty years of domestic US experience in supply chain operations. Upon her arrival in Seoul, she aggressively called a meeting and conveyed her agenda—as she would have done in the US. She wanted to have the solution in place within 48 hours and demanded a full report from each of the local executives that afternoon. None of the executives showed up for the afternoon meeting. When the US executive went from office to office looking for the summoned executives, she discovered they could not be found. In addition, none of the emails she sent to the Korean team were acknowledged. As her frustration level escalated, she pounded her fist on desks and loudly demanded staff members tell her where she could find the team. All of the secretaries cowered away from the American executive and many acted as if they could not speak English or understand her. After a ten day stay and no progress, she returned home. A week after her departure, the supply chain glitch was rectified by the Korean cohort and business resumed as normal.

As you can surmise, there were several mistakes made in this scenario. The female executive, selected to rectify the international challenge, approached the situation with little cultural sensitivity. It would take two days just to establish a relationship and a foundation for communication. The American approach of identifying the problem and instructing a team to quickly fix the glitch simply doesn't work in Korea. In addition, sending a tall, large, loud, strong-featured woman with a red bouffant is completely counter intuitive to the Korean business gender, appearance, and attire norm. It sabotaged any sense of familiarity and created a wall of distrust. And finally, in typical non-confrontational Korean style, the Korean team simply avoided and shut out the foreign participant until she finally left in frustration. However, in due time, and on their own timetable and their own way of operating within a group, the Korean team solved the problem.

The truth is there are a number of cultural ways to approach challenges and accomplish goals. It involves simply being aware, devising an approach that takes into consideration cultural norms and then strategizing accordingly. Select your negotiating or international team with precision. Pick your most culturally savvy players to represent you and keep in mind — in certain situations, especially when dealing with an older, established company or leadership team — you may have to lean towards a traveling male staff. I am not suggesting excluding women, however women selected for the team have to recognize they may play a secondary or deferential role. Fortunately, it appears women's roles in Asia are starting to evolve and from all indications, evolve quickly. Very soon I predict Chinese women will be a major force in the business arena. A few years ago, while facilitating cultural orientations, I noticed only a handful of Asian women in US business schools. However, in the last year, the number of Asian women—in particular, Chinese women—has risen dramatically. Now I see an even split between male and female Chinese students. China is, without a doubt, in the midst of a transition and although the degree of change is unpredictable, many savvy international gurus envision a full national renaissance.

The Chameleon Factor

As noted earlier in this chapter there is one key factor emerging in the big picture of taking your cultural knowledge to the next level. The key to building bridges in a multicultural world is through education, understanding your audience and respecting how you are perceived, then adapting your behavior accordingly—much like a *chameleon* which changes colors in order to survive. You can build rapports and levels of trust by adjusting your actions, dress, body language and voice tone to put others at ease. The more you make others feel comfortable, the stronger your relationships and your success rate will become.

A friend from college is a perfect example of how a cultural chameleon can thrive in the business world. He had carved out a middle-class existence as a real estate agent in Long Island. In 2007, when the real estate bubble exploded, he quickly became desperate. His business had fallen apart—he had no listings or buyers. Since his income is completely commission-based and the real estate market showed no signs of recovery, he called me in a panic. I encouraged him to reframe his efforts and take advantage of the current real estate situation. In essence, takes lemons and make lemonade.

Knowing a weak domestic real estate market and weak dollar translated into amazing real estate bargains for international investors, I helped him recreate and position himself in order to appeal to the international market. He obtained a Manhattan office and address by finding a small office space, which he shared with other small business owners. He then pitched potential American sellers by assuring them he could get top dollar for their properties from foreign investors. They had nothing to lose in a stagnant domestic market and got on board. He then took out a series of calculated ads in foreign newspapers and pitched himself as the contact person and real estate authority for their US investment. He also researched the ins and outs of foreign investment in the US, how investors could minimize legal and governmental hassles and made transactions easy for buyers. Those buyers then told their friends and soon he was getting barraged with calls.

He then went into what I call cultural chameleon mode. He learned a number of greetings and key phrases in a variety of target market languages (he already spoke German). The result: interested clients felt at ease when they spoke with him. He practiced each phrase repeatedly until he spoke like a native with the proper inflection and accent. He researched each culture before clients arrived in New York City and knew appropriate gifts to offer (if any at all), cultural superstitions (colors, numbers) and details right down to what kind of car he would rent to show them properties (his Swedish clients were delighted he "owned" an upscale Volvo). In addition, he familiarized himself with each cultural food item and ordered for the group when attending ethnic restaurants.

Essentially, he did everything he could to make his clients feel like they were being pampered by and interacting with "one of their own." The real estate bust was the best thing that ever happened to him. His business became and still is today, an overwhelming success. And he is the first one to tell you it is because of his ability to adapt his personality to suit the sales situation and, in essence, be a cultural chameleon.

Chapter 5

Respectful Americans

So, you are entertaining international business clients or perhaps are taking your delegation abroad. What can you include in your briefing so you, your peers and your company are perceived as sophisticated and refined Americans?

1. Tone It Down

Yes, Americans are loud and we are often perceived as individuals who dominate interactions. Worldly and sophisticated individuals typically speak in hushed tones and relate well to active listeners. Only those you are speaking to should be able to hear your conversation—not those who surround you. Make your interactions less about you and more about them—lower the decibels on your speech pattern and talk less, listen more.

2. Slow Down

Although we, as Americans, perceive ourselves as productive and efficient, we are often seen by other cultures as decision makers who often move forward without having all the facts or a complete picture of the project. In addition, many players from non-direct communicating cultures feel compelled to establish a relationship based on trust before doing business. The pipe dream of scheduling an initial international meeting and striking a deal in the same day are not realistic in most other cultures. Invest the time and energy to develop a strong rapport based on competence and integrity before making your pitch. When interacting with individuals from indirect communicating cultures, speak slowly and clearly. However, be careful your tone and actions do not appear patronizing.

3. Become Comfortable With Silence

Since we tend to move at such a fast pace, Americans often misinterpret lulls in conversation as uncomfortable situations and we often respond by filling in the conversation with unnecessary babble. Meanwhile, indirect communicating cultures often perceive non-verbal communicative gaps as an opportunity to digest the earlier discussed material and ponder their response. Give them their space and squelch your natural desire to react. Take the time during lulls to focus on the other party and in particular, hone your skills to become more aware of body language. While these are very foreign concepts to Americans, the other parties' gestures and non-verbal reactions are often very insightful.

4. Become More Formal

Our culture is an informal one and we often approach other cultures based on the norms of our own—an all too common and big mistake. For example, one American executive decided to make an impact in Japan on his first visit abroad by greeting Japanese executives by their first name followed by a friendly slap on the back. The executive's friendliness collided with the more formal Japanese culture. Not unlike most Japanese, in Germany, individuals address others by their surnames until receiving permission to do otherwise and touching another in a social situation is considered inappropriate and invasive. Remember George W. Bush's social gaffe with Germany's Prime Minister Angela Merkel? Upon greeting her at a large conference, he called her Angie and started to rub her shoulders. She quickly cowered away in disgust. Err on the side of caution and enter each cross-cultural relationship in a formal, docile and respectful manner.

5. Lose The Attitude

As Americans, we are often perceived as arrogant and self-centered. We frequently display a covert and, not seldom, overt sense of entitlement and superiority. Embrace the notion of a level playing field and realize others hailing from different lands may have a better approach to challenges. Become a true global leader who is aware of ethnocentric tendencies, respects others and embraces global best practices. Send signals communicating that you are open and want to embrace and learn about other cultures. One of the best ways to go about this is to make sure you don't rely on others to speak English with you. Learn and practice the basics in other languages—hello, goodbye, thank you, please, and other basics.

Chapter 6

Uniting Your Team

Now you are in the groove. You have a global mindset and feel comfortable with cross-cultural dynamics. It's time to get the best from your team—regardless of nationality or ethnicity—through culturally-sensitive focus groups. As a result of participating in this vital brain storming session, your organization will have developed a facet of business crucial to success: Global Best Practices.

How do you determine if culturally-sensitive focus groups are something your organization needs? Ask yourself the following questions as a barometer:

1. Does your team leave innovation to a certain department without input from groups that work directly with your customers?

2. Are your best managers and staff increasingly restless and cynical because they aren't being given the opportunity to shape your company's future?

3. If you asked a series of employees what they thought management considered fruitful areas for innovation, would you get a slew of different responses?

4. When you talk of employee-generated innovation with your team, do they act dismissively?

5. Does your management team think it's too costly and disruptive to hold regular focus groups or innovation discussions?

If you answered "yes" to all or most of these questions, you are ready to embark on a culturally-sensitive focus group program.

Fresh ideas and approaches save companies money while enhancing future leadership, growth and profits. Move towards Global Best Practices.

Global Best Practices sets the stage for:

- Greater consistency and standards,

- Increased service quality, customer impact and market branding

- Heightened employee engagement, morale and job satisfaction.

- Attracting and retaining top talent

- Clear expectations/unified culture

Now we take the big leap. It's time to gather the star organizational players and tap into their expertise. The individuals who do the work every day know better than anyone how to make the organization more efficient and customer focused. Chapter 7 puts the key program all together for you.

Chapter 7

We Are 1

Now you've determined your team is ready for a focus group. It's time to make it work.

The following outlines my culturally-sensitive focus group program, WEARE1. The WEARE1 program moves teams of diverse participants into a more involved experience, making Global Best Practice a well-tailored work of growth and discovery.

WEARE1

W - Who are the Participants? (Pre-work)

Prior to the training, the facilitator emails each participant an identical file. In addition to a program overview and focus group objectives, the file contains business, cultural and social traits that characterize all participating cultures in the upcoming international focus group. Global participants are asked to review the information and ask themselves two questions:

1. Does the description of your culture reflect your interactive style?

2. Are there other cultures represented in the exercise you believe you may have trouble working alongside?

In addition to the option of calling or contacting the facilitator to confidentially discuss any concerns, participants are asked to anonymously submit topics directly to the program assistants. The topics could be about departmental inconsistencies/obstacles, tools your department is lacking to do the job properly, or any other relevant concern. In addition to acknowledging current "problem areas," building upon the department's strengths is encouraged and participants are asked to think about positive and constructive solutions they will present during the program. Each "problem" is put on a "red brick." The red bricks are taped to the wall when participants enter the training room. The wall comes down later in the program when we "Entertain a Plan."

E - Encourage Dialogue (45 minutes)

The culturally savvy facilitator needs to accomplish two things:

1. Set the tone for honest communication

   - By stating clearly: "Although the organization is an American company, we are a global entity, what you do here will help decide the direction of your department.", "The company needs your input.", "Nobody knows your job better than you.", "This is a wonderful opportunity to make the organization an international and industry leader, etc."

2. Establish boundaries

   - The facilitator focuses on constructive input—if there is a problem, offer a solution, what we say here stays here, be respectful of other opinions.

Also, following a short culturally-based ice breaker, the facilitator generates a conversation around cultural descriptions communicating that it's impossible to put all of us from one single culture into a "box," but that there seem to be some common traits amongst members of each group. And then the facilitator inquires, "Was the description of your culture accurate?"

A - Acknowledge Hurdles (45 minutes)

The facilitator reviews the four major hurdles to obtaining global best practices via diverse, multicultural teams:

1. *Communication styles* (direct vs. indirect communicators),

2. *Language fluency/ability* (native English speakers vs. non-native English speakers — "You have been chosen for your task expertise, not for your fluency level."),

3. *Perceptions of hierarchy/authority* ("If you are uncomfortable participating in an American-style group, it's

understandable; however, we need your input. Come see the facilitator during the next break so the two of you can generate a plan."),

4. *Conflicting norms for decision makers* ("Americans are known for making quick decisions - your cultural approach may be different.").

The facilitator makes sure to offer several examples, asking group participants for their experiences, exploring how they overcame the hurdles, how everyone can best come together as a team and build on the group's strengths.

Break (15 minutes)

R - Restructure - if necessary (15 minutes)

At this juncture, the facilitator may decide to restructure the large group into smaller groups to reduce interpersonal friction or remove a source of conflict. Restructuring the dynamics of the group becomes necessary if the facilitator senses team members are defensive, threatened, or clinging to negative stereotypes of one another.

E - Entertain a Plan (90 minutes)

The facilitator reads each red brick to either one large or a series of small groups, depending on the circumstances, then clarifies the feedback. A summary/synopsis is later prepared for corporate decision makers.

1 - One Team and The Importance of Ongoing Collaboration (15 minutes)

Encourage team members to stay in touch, share information, exchange emails and work together in order to maintain the highest standards.

Chapter 8

Understanding China

A business book in today's economy would not be complete without a chapter on China. China is a huge potential market for American business. However, as mentioned, Chinese business norms are very different from US business norms, and therefore, require an investment of time and energy.

Accepting an invitation to visit a university or place of business in China presents numerous opportunities for considerable success or embarrassment. The difference between those two extremes—success or embarrassment—is defined by the level of investment made beforehand in understanding Chinese cultural expectations.

For example, several years ago, I accepted an invitation to present at a university in Shanghai. During my two-day visit, I counted over 30 potential cultural gaffes I could have easily made as a westerner.

Many Americans are aware of the business basics in China, such as how to present a business card (with both hands, palms up) and how to receive a business card (one should admire the card and thank the card's owner several times). However, the rituals are so much more in depth—for example, the significance of seating at a banquet (Chinese hosts typically arrange a "banquet" or dinner party in an impressive venue for visitors), appropriate gifts for hosts (upscale pen sets go over very well), how those gifts should be wrapped (certain colors only) and presented, the significance of receiving a gift, how one should react upon receiving the gift, when and how to toast hosts at a banquet, and when to return a toast. The protocol requirements go on and on, extending well beyond those mentioned here. Although the opportunities for social gaffes seem endless, you can navigate hurdles more easily by hiring a coach or doing your own homework and then segue into cultural chameleon mode. The more you make your hosts feel comfortable, the stronger your relationship will be.

Honor and Pride

Besides the rituals and protocol requirements, the level of honor and pride in the Chinese culture can be a surprising layer of distinction worth considering in order to understand the cultural mindset. The notion of "losing face" permeates many Asian cultures and Americans would be well-served to remember this fact. Beyond basic honor and pride, maintaining "face" avoids disgrace for the individual and their family, which is paramount in the Chinese culture.

During my work at a US university, I heard about a Chinese student who was caught in an unethical situation. He downloaded and copied an entire paper from the internet and submitted the work as his own. Because the paper was so well written and the professor knew the student's English was marginal, the professor did his own research on the internet and discovered the same paper the student submitted—word for word. Once the professor reported the incident, school leaders called in the student and confronted him. The student refused to admit he didn't write the paper. School authorities showed him the overwhelming evidence on the internet and yet, the student adamantly refused to admit he copied the paper. Most students would admit fault and ask for leniency when caught red handed, but this student would simply not back down. Even after he was released from the program and returned to China, he claimed he was wronged and a victim of a set up. But, if you understand the culture, this is not surprising. To admit he cheated and then was excused from the program would be a profound disgrace for both him and his family—so he had to stand by his story. Knowledge of these vital layers of Chinese cultural mores serves Americans well when approaching business or academic environments with the Chinese.

Besides respecting cultural protocol and other culture's values, it's important for Americans to know there are several ongoing obstacles when westerners do business in the world's largest emerging market. In addition, it is critically important for westerners to continually build and cultivate extensive networks of government and industry contacts who have the ability to help corporate projects and ventures succeed.

The following key points provide critical knowledge:

Business Challenges for Westerners in China

- Constantly shifting environment and contract aversion present unique challenges. Enforcement of rules and regulations in China vary widely by location and change without warning; partners routinely abandon contracts for better offers, and new competitors can become challenging foes seemingly overnight.

- A key to success lies in the development of quality relationships. Westerners must continually build and cultivate extensive networks of government and industry contacts in order to succeed.

- One of the biggest problems for western companies is unfair competition and poor protection of intellectual property rights.

- Identifying intermediaries or those who can open the applicable political doors or make strategic introductions (key to establishing trust and credibility) are in limited supply and often difficult to engage.

In a recent development, there is a distinct talent shortage—western and Chinese companies are seeking the same culturally savvy labor pool. Chinese companies are recruiting and enticing educated Chinese defectors to return home. In addition, many Chinese companies are now paying the same wages as multinational competitors.

American vs. Chinese Cultural Communication Mindset

We, as Americans, can learn much about the Chinese mindset and their ways of thinking, which will go a long way to understanding the corporate environment.

Let's look at contrasting ways of thinking, negotiating and reaching agreements:

1. American Individualism vs. Chinese Collectivism

Americans focus more on individual accomplishments versus the Chinese priority of focusing on the group and what is best for all.

2. American Egalitarianism vs. Chinese Hierarchical

As mentioned earlier, in general, Americans believe all members of a team are equal while the Chinese culture is highly hierarchical and those who are older and well educated are considered to have more experience and wisdom. Thus, young executives look to the elder statesman (in very rare cases, stateswoman, although the role of women in business is slowly evolving) to set the tone, decide if a working relationship will be formed or move forward and make major strategic decisions.

3. American Information Oriented vs. Chinese Relationship Oriented

Americans focus more on information—i.e. questioning whether the data support a strategic initiative. The Chinese, on the other hand, initially do not put as much emphasis on the actual deal but rather focus on individuals and their related personality traits. Although Americans will do business if the deal is perceived as a wise decision, Chinese want to know if the people they are doing business with are honest, ethical and to be trusted.

4. American Sequential Thought Process vs. Chinese Circular Thought Process

Americans are taught from a young age to be logical and sequential by focusing on ROI (Return On Investment). The A + B = C approach. However, the Chinese are circular in their thought process. This can be particularly frustrating for American sales teams since the Chinese often come back to renegotiate points Americans believe have already been discussed, settled and agreed upon.

5. American Value: "Seek the Truth" vs. Chinese Value: "Seek the Way"

Americans look for the "right" answer or decision and the quickest way to get to it. However, the Chinese believe there is value in evaluating and learning from the journey. The Chinese prefer to proceed slowly and pay keen attention to what "unfolds" along the way.

6. American "Argument Culture" vs. Chinese "Haggling Culture"

Americans believe in presenting their argument logically and based on facts. The Chinese have a different approach and believe in haggling. Interactions may be rooted in long periods of silence (which typically make Americans very uncomfortable) and lengthy negotiation. The Chinese are not necessarily interested in an American fact filled pitch (cost, profit margins, etc.) or rationale for taking a certain position. Rather, the Chinese will prolong interactions and negotiations in an attempt to get the best deal. The reality — the tactic often works with Americans who become quickly frustrated and present a more favorable package in order to close the deal. Unfortunately for impatient Americans, the tactic often backfires since the Chinese have the new favorable terms as a benchmark to once again begin haggling.

7. Quick American Meetings vs. Long Chinese Courting Process

Americans are accustomed to quick, productive meetings. The individual personalities or the players are not typically an issue. As long as a deal can be struck and a contract signed, most Americans are not concerned with the other side's personality traits or values. However, the Chinese business culture is focused on the relationship and the belief that one cannot forge a meaningful relationship quickly. With little pressure and an unlimited timeframe, the Chinese team is constantly observing and it's important to note, typically after each cross-cultural encounter, the Chinese delegation assembles and discusses their observations of the individual westerner or team.

8. Informal vs. Formal

Americans are notorious for being informal and often sense they have built an "addressing each other by first names" friendly relationship. However, in a business interaction, addressing a Chinese individual by first name is considered disrespectful and rude. In fact, it would behoove American executives to err on the side of caution and always address others formally. If someone wants you to call them by their first name, they will let you know. In China, formality and protocol are signs of respect and proper etiquette. The rationale: foreigners who are well bred will know how to conduct themselves properly.

9. Make Cold Calls vs. Draw On Intermediaries

In America, cold calls are the norm. If a sales person can anonymously find an individual or company that needs the product or service and a deal can be struck, all is well. However, the Chinese place great value on the business relationship and want to do business only with others who have credibility. Therefore, Americans who want to do business in China must find a suitable intermediary who carries clout with the Chinese client. The process to striking a deal is typically long. Not only does the American have to invest energy and time into forging a relationship with the client, often they must spend an even greater amount of time convincing the intermediary they are worthy of doing business.

10. Full Authority vs. Limited Authority

American sales representatives often have the ability to individually strike a deal. They know their product or service along with their cost and profit margins. Although the Chinese individual (or more often, individuals) who meets with the American executive may have the same product knowledge, the Chinese executive(s) will rarely single handedly make a deal. Rather, in true collective form, the Chinese liaison(s) will report back to their cohort with all the information and the group will tirelessly review every detail, including personal perceptions of the foreign executive (assessed level of trust, integrity, etc.).

11. Direct vs. Indirect Communication Styles

As mentioned in the earlier section, both cultures possess very different communication styles and are on the extreme ends of the cultural communication spectrum. In the past, Chinese exposure to western business was very limited, so, if a deal was to be struck, it was typically the American executive who had to adjust their behavior. However, there appears to be more compromise on the Chinese side as international exposure and awareness regarding American business norms increases. In addition, the Chinese have become motivated as their manufacturing and export levels exponentially increase.

12. Proposals First vs. Explanations First

Americans can get off to a poor start if they jump right into proposals when trying to forge a business relationship with indirect communicators, including the Chinese. Rather, it is imperative to make the first few interactions about protocol and building a personal relationship built on trust and respect. During interactions, the Chinese want to hear about your motives, better understand your business history and generalities about why a business relationship is beneficial for both parties. Proposals and details follow later—much later.

13. Aggressive vs. Questioning

Americans relish productivity and like to keep the negotiation process moving. However, the Chinese prefer to let the process unfold and typically ask a series of open-ended questions in an attempt to better understand American players and motive.

14. Impatient vs. Enduring

As the relationship develops, many Americans become impatient. After a series of meetings and several months of dialogue, Americans often wonder if the investment of time and energy will pay off.

The Chinese, on the other hand, are often content going slowly and meticulously. They do not want to enter a relationship they may later regret. Before they can move towards an agreement, they must fully understand the players and feel comfortable with the interactions. In the US, we have a familiar adage, *"Time is money."* In China, time and money are always separate. *Time is time and money is money.*

15. Forging a "Good Deal" vs. Forging a "Long Term Relationship"

Americans tend to focus on the here and now. Strike the deal and move on to the next one. However, the Chinese are focused on an ongoing long-term relationship. They invest the time and energy on the front end to identify and find the best fit. They seek long-term partners for ongoing business. The upside: if you can strike a deal after a long and arduous process—you have high hopes of return business or additional business through referral.

Chapter 9

Understanding the Middle East

Of course there are a number of misunderstood cultures and it would be impossible to highlight all the global misconnects in this book. However, in my experience, Arabs rank right at the top of the culturally misunderstood list. It's important to include a glimpse into this predominant Middle Eastern group in order to round out the global education experience.

In 2005, I wrote my first book and found myself first on a domestic book tour and then, shortly thereafter, on an international book tour. My trip was a whirlwind and eventually I found myself in Dubai. The two Emirati hosts assigned to accompany me to different television and radio stations for interviews were very friendly. I immediately liked both of them and found them to be especially funny, hospitable and disarming. After a long day of interviews, they offered to take me to one of their favorite restaurants for dinner.

As we dined on a charming outdoor patio overlooking the skyscrapers cascading over the desert oasis, one of the gentlemen caught me off guard. He turned to me and with a broad grin, asked, "So Bill, what do Americans think about Arabs?" I often answer a question with a question. (My father always taught me a lesson I have employed over and over many times in my life—if someone ever asks you a question you are uncomfortable answering, always respond with a question. The strategy buys you time while you gather your thoughts.) So after a few seconds, I smiled and said, "Well, what do Arabs think about Americans?" Both of my hosts laughed and said, "You go first and then we will tell you."

I felt comfortable with these two chaps, so I decided to be forthcoming. I said, "If you were to ask Americans what they think about

Arabs, many would say Arabs are religious extremists, actually Muslim extremists."

Both hosts laughed out loud and one said, "That is what we think about you. Many Arabs think America is full of Christian extremists."

We all shifted in our seats, "Tell us something else," they said with broad smiles.

I thought for a brief moment and said, "Many Americans think Arabs are disrespectful of women." My hosts looked at each other with slack jaws and one put his hands on the side of his head in disbelief. The other host stammered, "How can you say that? How can Americans possibly think that? Coming from a country with the highest rates of pornography, rape and domestic violence, how can you possibly say we disrespect women?" My mouth dropped and I was speechless. I had never thought about America in that context.

Our conversation comparing our cultures went on from there for several hours, discussing contrasting cultural approaches from marriage, child care and perceptions of the elderly to crime, punishment, sex and drugs. I felt like I was looking through the cultural lens of a telescope and that telescope swiveled around all night, enabling me to share perceptions of another culture while taking an honest look at my own.

Communicating Styles

Although it was clear to me mainstream Arabs and Americans actually had much more in common than many may surmise, there are distinct differences in the ways we communicate and relate to others within and outside our cultures. Arabs, in direct contrast to typical American communication styles and as discussed in previous material, much like Japanese and Chinese, are indirect communicators. However, unlike Asians, Arabs are talkative and engaging. In addition, Arabs tend to value eye contact while Asians are often visually avoidant.

Furthermore, Arabs tend to be a high context culture (as are Asian cultures) while Americans are a low context culture— meaning that Americans are specific, explicit and analytical while *traditional* Arabs tend to be vague, circular in thought and rarely verbalize their wants or needs clearly and directly. Now I clarified this statement by saying "traditional" because western educated Arabs in many parts of the Arab world are very direct. This is why, it is important to note, Arabs, like most groups who share a similar heritage, are impossible to universally characterize or label. Jordanians are very different than Kuwaitis who differ from Saudis. Then there is the French influence in countries like Lebanon, Algeria and Morocco, which impacts Arab interaction styles on a completely different level.

Additionally, there are many Arabs who are cultural chameleons in their own right. Arabs can be traditional in dress, manner and approach when doing business with a conservative Arab partner over lunch and then take on a western appearance in a suit and tie that same evening while discussing business with a westerner or another western-educated Arab.

There are other cultural misconnects between Americans and Arabs. Arabs, like many indirect communicators, often expect others to cue into the unspoken and understand what they are thinking based on subtle verbal hints or body language. Arabs will often talk around the main point they are hoping you grasp—without specifically or clearly stating their message. Their hope is the western listener will understand the covert message and then actually verbalize the meaning in a direct manner—indicating both parties are on the same page.

In effect, the burden of communication in the Middle East often falls on the western listener. This, of course is in direct contrast to American communication styles. If there is confusion or misunderstanding surrounding a message delivered in the US, the communicator is then seen as unable to effectively verbalize his or her thoughts—not the other way around.

Expectations

I have found there are underlying threads that connect the Arab world. An Arab business associate and I worked briefly on a project together. I considered our relationship a cordial short-term business relationship and an ongoing acquaintance who I spoke with infrequently. Yet, when this gentleman's son came to the US for college, the expectation level, on his part, was much greater. The business associate indirectly, (but in several different ways), requested I check in with his son regularly, invite his son to my home for weekend holiday breaks and all in all, be his guardian. I could tell by his voice and the words he chose during our phone conversation, he was not asking for a favor. Rather, because we had done business together and therefore had forged a bond, he connoted his expectation to me. From my American vantage point, I felt like this former colleague was asking a lot from me and overstepping his boundaries. However, I knew if I did not gratify his request and appear to happily offer to support his son, I would "burn a bridge" and jeopardize any future business links.

Additionally, the Arab approach to time and in particular, scheduling, is contrary to American norms. Arabs are often late, so it's best to take the entire experience in stride. If you have a meeting with an Arab associate at 11am, don't be surprised if the other party does not show up until early afternoon.

However, you should be at the agreed upon meeting spot at 11am. Just bring a book.

Another contrast between the two cultures is value related. Americans place high value on accomplishments and value achievements. Arabs tend to value hierarchy. An individual's family name and social status are of utmost importance. In other words, in the Arab world, it's not so much what you do, it's who you are.

Additionally, Arabs are circular thinkers and communicators, much like the Chinese, which of course, is perplexing and frustrating for Americans (discussed in previous chapter).

When interacting with Arabs, you have to employ flattery, and charm in order to achieve a level of rapport otherwise taken for granted. "My, what a beautiful home, delightful children, a scrumptious meal, a gorgeous country, an amazing culture." The more demonstrative and over the top you are with praise, the better. Discreet and reserved westerners do not typically do well in the Arab world. Silence is perceived as arrogance. During the relationship building process, it is vital to be gregarious and engaging and offer compliments to your host, his company and his country in general.

You, in return, will be complimented, which often leads to the next step in the interaction. After the initial bonding, the next stage of the relationship starts with what I call the inquisition and it often comes with a slew of questions that often makes us, as westerners, uncomfortable. How much money do you make? What is your religion? By the way, if you are an atheist, don't admit it, it will not go over well and will lead to suspicion. Are you married and if so, is this your only marriage? How many children do you have? In other words, boundaries are non-existent and you should be ready for just about any question. The most important thing to remember: take the inquisition in stride and continue to smile.

If you are working on a project, don't expect to be told if the project is not going smoothly or is behind deadline. Like many indirect communicators, Arabs do not like to convey bad news, disappoint you or have you think poorly of their abilities. So if you want to know the reality of a situation, ask questions that require elaborate answers (Tell me the details about the project) vs. a yes/no question (Is the project going well?).

Although Americans are often perceived as loud, Arabs are often perceived as even louder. Take it in stride—it's actually a good thing. It means your Arab colleague is engaged in the conversation.

Another example of fluid boundaries: You may be in the midst of a meeting with an Arab on his turf when suddenly the door opens and another Arab business person enters the office. They may have a conversation for several minutes. This typically throws westerners for a loop. Relax, smile and go with the flow—your conversation will resume in due time.

And finally, don't forget to maintain eye contact. According to the culture, a man's sincerity and honor can be judged by their ability to look you in the eye.

The bottom line: we see booming economies and state-of-the-art hospitals, airlines, universities and multinational corporations in once remote locations like Dubai, Abu Dhabi and Doha. Those economies, fueled by petroleum-related revenues, will offer tremendous opportunity well into the future. Finesse your cultural chameleon presentation and make it work for you. You can do it.

Chapter 10
Understanding India

Although India has faded from the limelight of international business, the unique culture is one worth understanding.

Starting in the late 1990's, many international gurus predicted an economic boom and unlimited opportunities in India. It was considered one of the most promising emerging markets, mainly due to a huge population base and predictions of a growing middle class. Many predicted the Indian consumer market would explode and business opportunities would grow exponentially. To a large degree, the boom never materialized with a series of fits and starts and international entrepreneurs and corporations sought more promising ventures in other parts of the world. However, several analysts predict India will come roaring back. The potential is there amongst millions of consumers, but the obstacles inherent in the culture, primarily the caste system, have thus far, kept the economy from moving forward and capitalizing on its potential.

Social Structure and Obstacles

In India, there is a distinct societal obstacle that hinders teamwork and progress. In essence, there is no rolling up your sleeves and jumping in to get the job done. Everyone is well aware of societal position and societal rules dictate Indians only perform work that is deemed appropriate for their social position. This hierarchical system permeates every aspect of Indian life, including business relationships, family interactions and even friendships. In fact, the sense of hierarchy is so strong that it even affects interactions with strangers.

Every relationship involves hierarchies. In schools, teachers are considered gurus and are perceived as all knowing. The family patriarch, typically the father, is the undisputed leader of the family. The boss is seen as solely responsible for the business. Each and every relationship has a clear-cut hierarchy with corresponding roles and those roles are rarely, if ever questioned.

The government and established gate keeper for progress is a keen illustration. First of all, most government officials are political appointees from privileged families and often do not have the skill set or experience to lead their departments. Although this kind of payoff occurs in other countries, including the US, it is considered an across-the-board cultural norm in India, often resulting in bureaucratic chaos. In addition, the cultural norm is not to take responsibility for errors or mistakes. It is shameful to not appear competent, so the culture is riddled with blame and little accountability. It's a recipe for lots of commotion and drama, but, all too often, little progress. And that is only one of many obstacles to progression.

For example, an American friend and project manager relayed his experience to me. He was in India for a meeting with government officials. At this particular meeting, there were four more attendees than available conference room seats. Instead of simply swinging in another table and four chairs from an adjoining conference room, a low class laborer was called to move the furniture. However, that worker was on another job and since he did not want to say he could not do the job (Indians rarely say no—there is a fear and aversion to disappoint, especially those from a higher social strata), he did not arrive to move the one table and four chairs for almost an hour. Meanwhile, in an effort to get the meeting on track, the American offered to move the furniture himself and was told absolutely not. As the American fidgeted and looked at the clock, the other participants made idle chit chat and genially socialized. When the worker arrived, the mood shifted and the attendees assaulted the worker with a series of verbal insults. After the worker moved the table and chairs (which took no more than a minute), the laborer was then seemingly punished for his behavior and told to move the furniture back since there was now no time for the meeting (which by the way, the fiasco was deemed the worker's fault and he was verbally abused for several minutes before he fled the room). At that juncture, the lead manager declared the meeting would be scheduled for another unspecified time in the future and he then announced he was heading home to tend to a family emergency (Families are paramount in Indian society and take precedence over all other situations. If a meeting is canceled, a "family emergency" is often the reason provided.). The attendees loudly continued to degrade the worker and followed the leader out of the room. Struggling to digest what had just taken place, the American was aghast and had no idea how to proceed.

These kinds of cross-cultural misconnects not only afflict the business environment in India, but also affect other venues. While facilitating graduate school orientations, I readily observe cross-cultural group dynamics and once again, social class and privilege amongst Indian students often comes into play. Typically in an American group environment, everybody is expected to participate and work assignments are shared. However, I often see Indian participants assume a supervisory perspective and expect other group members to do the actual work.

As a result, group members from other cultures sometimes perceive Indians as lazy or entitled. But that is not the case. Rather, it's a cultural misconnect. Indian students studying in the US are only from the highest social classes and thus, many of them have not worked in the trenches, so to speak. As a result of their societal norm, doing the actual work is perceived as subordinate and inappropriate for someone of their stature. It's simply a part of the societal fabric, which, based on egalitarian American values, typically bewilders, frustrates and even angers Americans. However, once Americans understand the Indian caste system and cultural norm, multicultural groups can devise strategies to create understanding and bridge the gap.

Several years ago, I was asked to facilitate a cross-cultural intervention on a major college campus. A group of Indian students had outraged university front line staff and a series of verbal spats had erupted between the two groups. The staff who handle the day-to-day paperwork, updating transcripts and collecting fees, felt demeaned by Indian students. As a result of Indian students tossing their paperwork at them and addressing them arrogantly, the staff considered the behavior of the group of Indian students disrespectful and condescending.

As I contemplated how to build a bridge of understanding between the two warring groups, I opted for a culturally empathic approach as a remedy for healing and peace between the two factions. I arranged a meeting and invited both groups to attend. Once in the same room, I then outlined the caste system to the group and discussed the American value of equality and mutual respect. I then asked each group to understand the other culture's expectations and find a way to interact and function together. As we delved deeper into the issues, I encouraged the American administrators not to personalize the behavior. The students' behavior was not an attack on them in particular, but rather the cultural perception of their professional role. In addition, I reminded the students they are in the US and should respect the host country's expectation of being polite to all, regardless of perceived social class. Although there was no love lost between the groups by the end of the session, they understood the other perspective and were able to forge a stilted, yet cordial rapport for the remainder of the school year.

India's Middle Class and Customer Service History

Although India, in relation to the overall population, has a tiny upper class and overwhelming poverty amongst the masses, there is evidence of a growing middle class and that middle class group is well educated. In fact, based on the perception of an abundance of quality and cost effective Indian employees, American companies saw an opportunity in the late 1990's. By establishing customer service centers in India for American companies, many American leaders envisioned a way to cut labor costs and maintain service levels. The strategy was seen as advantageous on many levels. In particular, in addition to employing multi-lingual and versatile Indian talent to replace costly American customer service representatives, many American leaders foresaw an Indian middle class that would grow exponentially, thus creating profitable opportunities for multinational corporations.

Although the endeavor seemed logical and viable, cross-cultural customer service norms were not considered and for many companies, the effort was a disaster. Although Indian staffers spoke English well, communication gaps between Indian phone representatives and American consumers became immediately evident. Americans not only speak quickly, but often use slang which was lost in translation. In addition, American consumers expected customer service glitch resolutions to be resolved on the spot, which is counter intuitive to Indian business culture. As the culture dictates, Indian workers followed service manuals to the letter and do not deviate from policy. If the exact customer service challenge was not outlined in the manual, American consumers with unique requests were immediately referred to a supervisor who would typically put the consumer on hold. Since the answer was not in the manual, initial representatives would then send the consumer to a higher ranking supervisor and so on. As you can imagine, American consumers became irate and complaints soared. As a result, many of these customer service centers have now closed and yet another opportunity for India has vanished.

In spite of the historical challenges and setbacks, there are a number of reasons to understand this unique culture. One, circumstances change and if the massive potential market in India evolves, there will be countless opportunities. And two, you will be better able to understand and effectively interact with the growing number of Indian communities in the US and abroad.

General Business Protocol

India is one of the most fascinating and complex cultures in the world with close to 30 different regions—including a myriad of different religions, languages and social protocols. However, most international business, at least for now, is conducted with a particular social class in the urban centers of Delhi, Mumbai, Bangalore and Hyderabad. So for the purpose of this chapter, we will focus on that population. Although Hindi is the country's official language, the effects of British colonialism are still evident and

English is the language of international business.

Like the Chinese, Indians prefer to do business with individuals they know and trust. Consequently, making introductions through a well-respected third party or intermediary is helpful.

Indian business etiquette resembles British formality. Requests for meetings should be well in advance, generally at least a month. As stated before, "family emergencies" often arise and meetings are canceled on short notice, so reconfirm your meeting the week before and again the morning of the meeting. Remain flexible for last minute changes and be punctual (Although Indians typically run late, foreigners are expected to be on time.). Don't be surprised if the first one or two meetings include little business talk. At that time, you are being assessed and evaluated to see if you are a good personal fit and appear trustworthy. For future meetings and in order to move forward, you have to set the stage and guide the process. If you don't set the tone, the process will often languish. Send a detailed agenda in advance. In addition, send all supporting materials, including charts, data, marketing plans and other related material. Follow up your meeting with an overview of what was discussed and the steps to follow. If you don't take the lead, the chances of moving forward diminish greatly.

Indians expect discounts and concessions in both price and terms. Many seasoned international business veterans simply pad their initial prices and terms with this in mind. Regarding attire, always convey respect by dressing conservatively. Although the weather is often exceedingly hot and humid, you typically have to sweat it out in a proper suit.

Indians love titles. If you are a professor, doctor, engineer or any other professional with a title, you can use this to your advantage. Status is determined by caste, profession, university degree and age — typically in that order. If no title is evident, address others by Sir or Madam. If someone prefers to be addressed by their first name, they will let you know. Business cards are vital and exchanged at the first meeting after the initial handshake. Unlike the Chinese who use both hands to present their business card, only use your right hand and present the card so the type faces the Indian recipient. As one would do in China, you may print your information on the back of your card in the host language (Hindi). Additionally, take a moment to admire the card and make sure you treat the card with respect—admire it again and convey thanks before placing the card gingerly in your front shirt pocket (never in the back pocket of your slacks).

Communicating Styles

Indians are non-confrontational (in typical indirect communicating style). Decisions are reached by the person with the most authority and power. As you can surmise, decision making is often a painfully slow process. But be patient—if you lose your temper, you will lose face and prove you are unworthy as a business partner and hence, you will not be respected or trusted. When negotiating, avoid a hard sell or high pressure approach. If you are remotely confrontational or even perceived as overly assertive, you will blow the deal. Criticisms and disagreements should be expressed lightly, diplomatically and with little emotion.

Remember, Indians have an aversion to saying "no" as it is culturally inappropriate to disappoint or offend. Listen carefully to responses to your questions. If you hear words like "We'll see," "I will try" or "possibly," then chances are you are politely being told 'no.'

Social Basics

India has many religions—Hindus, Muslims, Sikhs and even Catholics—all with their own distinct sets of norms, values and societal rules. So here are some basics that will not offend any group.

1. Men typically shake hands with men and women shake hands with other women; however men and women often do not shake hands.

2. Wait for a person of the opposite sex to indicate their comfort zone. If a hand is extended, shake it. If not, do not make any overtures.

3. Socially, always address the most prestigious person first when entering a meeting or restaurant and only discuss safe topics like business or sports.

4. Avoid talking about personal issues as they are often interpreted as boastful or self-consumed.

5. Although poverty and beggars are prevalent in India, avoid the topic altogether or you may appear arrogant.

6. If you are invited to someone's home, you may want to remove your shoes before entering the home (discreetly look down as the front door opens and take the lead from the host).

7. Presenting a host with a gift can be tricky turf. Like the Chinese, many Indians are superstitious. It's often difficult to remember which gifts and colors are appropriate when on a multi-stop international trip, hopping from country to country. I always have a number of Mont Blanc pens wrapped in red paper. It's a universally well-received and safe gift. By the way, your gift will rarely be opened in front of you and, if you receive a gift, thank the host profusely and open the package when you get back to your hotel. Then upon seeing the host after the initial gift

exchange, thank them again, at least twice.

The most important part of your business interaction is not necessarily the product or service you are offering. Rather, it is how you are perceived. If you are humble, respectful, incredibly patient and follow social protocol, you will be well on your way to a solid business relationship since this is the first step and integral part of forging a deal in India.

Chapter 11
Your Career Path

So now you are a bona fide "Citizen of the World" and want to interview for an exciting new position as a global leader. What questions can you expect and how can you prepare?

Following are five of the most often asked interview questions and samples of culturally savvy responses for you to consider.

1. What did you learn most from your previous position(s)?

In my current position as _____, I worked with a variety of peers from different cultures. In addition to gaining valuable practical experience in _____, I had the opportunity to manage multicultural teams and as a result, learned how to effectively communicate and lead key players who hail from cultures different than my own.

2. Why do you want to work for our company?

I see your company not only as a leader in the industry, but also as a globally focused organization that is positioned well to expand internationally. I am confident of my ability to interact with peers from around the world and will thrive in your company culture.

3. What would you say is your biggest accomplishment in your career/life? Why?

I see my biggest accomplishment as my ability to expand my perspective. I have put a tremendous amount of energy into overcoming any sense of ethnocentrism I may have harbored and am open to other cultural approaches. In addition, I am familiar with the hurdles to cross-cultural communication and am confident in my ability to overcome culturally based communication obstacles. As a result, I am a solid team player and considered a strong leader.

4. How would you describe your personality?

I would characterize myself as open minded, competent and flexible. In a nutshell, I work well both individually and in a group setting. In particular, I enjoy working with a diverse group of peers and am a respected liaison, who is known to build camaraderie and unify teams.

5. How would you describe your interaction style in groups?

I thoroughly enjoy group projects and in particular, I thrive in multicultural group settings and believe in achieving global best practices. During my time at (blank) company, I have had the opportunity to participate in a number of cross-cultural projects and facilitated cross-cultural focus groups.

You are ready to soar in the global marketplace. You have not only the tools to initiate a personal culture transformation, but a departmental and organizational renaissance. You have the opportunity to impact your company and position your organization for an increasingly interactive global marketplace. By following the timeline outlined in this publication, you will witness a rapid transition.

Now it's time to consider one more layer to round out your transition and cultivate an internal environment to ensure long-term sustainable cross-cultural awareness and sensitivity.

Chapter 12
Opening Our Minds

Of course you are a unique and intelligent leader who wants to learn and have been drawn to this book. You aren't just a sharp business persona, but a human being who may or may not make critical decisions based on your personal thoughts. So it benefits you to know who you are and why you think what you think. The question to dwell on for this chapter is "How open-minded am I?"

This question is by no means a criticism or judgment. I find it interesting how people automatically react when discussing prejudice, bias or racism. The immediate and politically correct response is: "I'm not prejudiced." But it's just not true. All of us are prejudiced and there is no shame in harboring prejudices. All of us learned various thoughts and attitudes about other groups as we matured. But we can elevate ourselves to a higher plane by acknowledging our prejudices, identifying where they came from and then make a conscious effort to open our minds. To that end, I've devised a three-step process.

The exercise is a worthy investment of your energy and will quickly move you down the "Citizen of the World" experience curve and firmly entrench both feet on the ground as a centered, self-aware global leader.

Open the door to shedding prejudice with the following three-step process:

1. Acknowledge

The first step is quite easy. You just have to acknowledge you are human and that, as an inevitable fact of being human, you harbor prejudice and are willing to embark on a journey to rid yourself of restricting and/or negative thoughts about other groups of people.

2. Trace

The second step is to trace what you think about other groups and identify what your conscious or subconscious may feel about groups or individuals who may have different backgrounds than you. For the purposes of this book, circle the globe and think about ethnicities different than your own. Then start generating a list from all continents (ex: Swedes, Thais, Nigerians, Mexicans, and Australians) and write down the first reaction (without filters—you will be the only one to see your responses) that enters your mind when you think of these groups.

3. Explore and Challenge

The third step dives even more thoroughly into your self-analysis. Ask and answer two critical sets of questions as shown in the following in order to explore and challenge prejudice:

> ➢ Where did my thoughts about others originate and become engrained in my mind? Did they come from my family of origin? Media? Community? Church? Did I pick them up in my own personal interactions? Did they enter into my thinking via another source?

> ➢ How can I take myself to a higher plane and become more open to the amazing and talented diversity in our world? Is it fair to draw conclusions about the behavior of others based on stereotypes? How can I identify and appreciate the best others have to offer? Even if other groups behave differently than I do, am I willing to put the human tendency towards ethnocentrism aside and become open to the idea that another approach or thought process might actually be a better fit?

Although this is a short chapter and exercise, it is critical. Take the time and sit

with your thoughts. You will get out of it
what you put into it, and much more.

Chapter 13
Looking Ahead

Now is the ideal time to not only recap some of the book's highlights, but also to ask you to consider if other cultural approaches might, in fact, be more functional and superior to how you currently conduct yourself personally and professionally. This line of thinking or discussion may not be comfortable for you, depending on your ethnocentric barometer. But don't beat yourself up—regardless of our backgrounds, we are all ethnocentric and can afford to consciously challenge ourselves from time to time. Besides, isn't true global leadership what you want to strive towards? True global leaders have an expansive mindset and embrace Global Best Practices.

The following bits and pieces from earlier chapters allow me to give you my take and some additional fodder for you to ponder. They are presented here as nine different cultural considerations and conclude with what I'm referring to as cultural considerations on the flip side.

Cultural Consideration 1

"In fact, American leaders love innovation and often encourage their team to take risks. 'We tried that and it didn't work. Let's try another approach.' is not an uncommon attitude. Many German executives consider the American decision-making style as overly focused on productivity with too little emphasis on following a logical, strategic process and quality decision making." "And in Japan, the Japanese look at every decision from all angles before moving ahead."

Which culture's tactic is better and might it behoove American business to slow down and research repercussions of decisions from each and every angle before implementation?

Certainly reviewing a strategy from all angles would result in fewer strategic errors. However, many American leaders assert a slower pace and less risk would result in higher costs and less innovation. And realistically, America has not become a superpower by following the leads of others or resting on its laurels. American business is known for innovation and many of the country's discoveries have come about because leaders took a chance or followed a hunch. For many years, America's higher-than-average productivity level served the country well.

In spite of the seemingly positive implications for some companies, in my opinion and observations, productivity levels have soared past the point of maximal performance and have actually become counter-productive. The current corporate pace of American business is not sustainable and the data prove it. Only about one third of American workers are engaged at work. And US business is losing about $300 billion a year due to stress-related illness. As one of my

European friends recently told me, "America has become a sweat shop." Many American executives are simply burned out and as a result, poor decisions are being made—from the C- Suite on down the managerial food chain. Although difficult to quantify, one can only imagine the additional losses due to exhausted workers making poor decisions.

As a testament to a saner pace, well thought out decisions result in higher levels of quality as exemplified by German production quality and service levels. American business can increase quality of goods and services and increase employee satisfaction by getting off the frenetic treadmill, and encouraging a more balanced life. As productivity levels become unmanageable and overwhelming, work quality suffers. And not only is that a loss, but employees can only do three people's jobs for so long before the business starts to fray.

It makes me wonder—is our culture addicted to work? Unlike many other cultures, Americans typically self-identify through their career choice and their company. Our mindset often bewilders those from other cultures. My European friends think of their jobs as something they do, it does not make up who they are. In addition, Americans average on the low end of vacation time compared to other cultures — usually about two weeks per year. Yet, although receiving little time to regroup and relax, Americans, on average, don't take two days of vacation per year. When I worked in corporate America, much to my amazement, I recall a colleague insinuating my vacation choice (sailing in the Atlantic and unable to correspond with the home office for a week) was irresponsible. Vacation is a time to disconnect from work and rejuvenate.

A suggested tweak to the American corporate mindset: take all of your vacation, completely disconnect (yes, the company will survive without you), return to work rejuvenated, take the time to reconnect with family and friends and, upon returning to work, rededicate yourself to quality over productivity.

Cultural Consideration 2

"I can't begin to tell you the number of times I have facilitated cross-cultural focus groups and a brilliant participant has been dismissed or ignored because of their inability to verbalize their input

clearly in the host language. Americans are at a distinct advantage because many meetings are conducted in English."

Missing out on insightful input goes beyond language challenges. American executives are often missing out on valuable input from talented staff members (including non-native English speakers) who are not stationed at headquarters. Although American companies boast global divisions and worldwide reach, the reality reveals that American executives rarely have a global mindset and are often ethnocentric in attitude. Part of that narrow mindset includes overlooking the potential of educated and savvy employee groups in non-headquartered locales. The result: a lost opportunity to improve the company in a number of ways such as streamlining the operation or improving customer service—all leading to Global Best Practices.

In general, regardless of the country or the company, employees who are not based in the home office are overlooked. It's a natural "out of sight, out of mind" phenomenon, but can be overcome with a concerted effort at employee inclusion in the form of culturally and language sensitive focus groups. It's a worthy investment. In addition to valuable input, such an organizational endeavor builds bridges of unity throughout the system and sustains ongoing communication amongst diverse work groups.

Employees, who are removed from the daily political drama of home office politics, often have a keen and unique perspective of how the organization is succeeding or failing. Once again, the adage, "the minority knows more about the majority than the majority knows about itself" comes into play. In this case, often those who work outside headquarters know more about what works and doesn't work in the organization than those in the hub. Employees on the fringe are at a distinct advantage by not being embroiled in the political whirlwind and jockeying for position mindset that typically characterizes the interdepartmental home office environment. As a result of cross-cultural focus groups, leaders are typically amazed at the insightful and innovative ideas gleaned from these sessions. In addition, employees on the geographic fringe of the company feel more valued and connected to the organization.

Cultural Consideration 3

"...in a German company, every senior executive expects to be briefed and is expected to be up to speed about every aspect of the project—not just what is transpiring within their own department."

The German approach to project management, with clearly outlined goals and orderly layers of accountability, stems from the top down. On the other hand, most employees in corporate America see a more lax approach within American companies, resulting in a number of American divisional leaders juggling several endeavors, all with individual agendas, consequently creating a plethora of inconsistencies. You end up with wasted productivity and projects that don't always support overall company goals. Why does this happen? Often, there is a lack of vision from the top combined with a lack of clarity regarding how individuals and departments are meant to support company goals.

Adopting a more German-influenced approach insures leaders and employees alike have a clear "big picture" of the company's goals and how they are to be achieved. The no-nonsense reality of German business leaders is very clear and there are few opportunities to talk your way out of a departmental failure—all the way down the managerial line. You are effective and follow the CEO's mandate or you are out.

Cultural Consideration 4

"The Japanese have to establish trust and a relationship before expressing their opinion and engaging with a potential business partner. Additionally, Japanese executives feel they need to intuitively understand the players in the group."

According to many of my American colleagues, business is not a popularity contest and they don't feel the need to evaluate a business partner's ethics or know much about their personal lives. In addition, Americans feel protected by the legal system and in particular, the American emphasis on contracts, so striking a deal with someone of questionable integrity is not always concerning.

I understand this perspective and respect setting a limit, which separates a business relationship from a personal one. But shouldn't ethics be at least a consideration and a part of the conversation? Regardless of contractual protection and guaranteed compensation for work, do any of us really want to be affiliated with an underhanded individual or organization? What does that say to our employees, suppliers and other customers in the US and abroad about our level of integrity? Many cultures, particularly Asian cultures, will do exhaustive research on American suitors before conducting business. If they discover your affiliation with questionable partners, they will absolutely not do business with you. The bottom line — linking up with sly individuals or companies may benefit you in the short run, but is likely to cost you in the long run.

Cultural Consideration 5

"In fact, many American middle managers feel compelled to speak out when in the midst of senior executives. The mid-level players view the

opportunity as a chance to impress the senior executives. However, in more docile and laid back indirect communicating business cultures, members tend to take a more passive position, assess the players and selectively participate."

This is an interesting observation and speaks to the American tendency to value those who are outspoken, take center stage and personify charisma. The unfortunate result is twofold. One, all too often the outspoken individual, in an anxiety-provoked desire to make a positive impact, blurts out an inappropriate statement or comment, which in, a matter of seconds, sabotages their reputation. Additionally, some American executives habitually overlook the more reserved but brilliant future leaders who "talk less, listen more". I am putting my money on "Speak softly and carry a big stick" as a great mantra of future successful global leaders. In this case, to carry a big stick is to embody true global leadership, challenge the status quo and maintain accountability while listening more.

Cultural Consideration 6

"It would be considered disrespectful for a more junior person to disagree with a seasoned, senior member. And that attitude and sense of respecting elders and experience in the field permeates much of Asia."

Soliciting and valuing the input of an experienced and seasoned executive is often overlooked in American business. An American executive, in their mid- 50's, is often considered over the hill. Executives in this age group, well aware they are in a vulnerable place, often become skittish and avoid the limelight. The executive's goal at that career crossroad is, all too often, to stay below the radar until retirement. Additionally, many older executives are exhausted from the corporate pace and disillusioned with politics that permeate American corporations. What a waste of seasoned talent. Tap into this resource.

This may be a bit off track, but the following point is very illustrative. The discussion surrounding age reminds me of a cross-cultural experience I had in the Netherlands. I couldn't help but notice, while

124

on a business trip to Amsterdam, the anchors on one of the main news channels were not only very old, but seemingly unattractive—a direct contrast to news anchors in the US. When I noted the observation to my Dutch colleague, he very directly (as the Dutch do) told me his culture respects individuals for their intelligence while America values people for their youth and appearance. He pointed out the number one magazine sold in the US is People and our country regularly elects individuals to political positions based on their looks and charm, not their abilities or beliefs. What could I say? The sad reality is he is right. How can we move towards valuing depth, experience and knowledge?

It seems Americans could afford to consider the value of age and experience which is apparently not exclusive to Asia but, as evidenced by my own experience, flourishes in the Netherlands as well.

Cultural Consideration 7

"An American's 'take charge and organize the group' actions are often perceived by indirect communicators (in this case, the Japanese

participant)   as   overtly   aggressive   and dominating."

I see it time and time again. Americans feel compelled to take the lead, loudly perform in a multicultural setting and, so they think, charm business leaders from other cultures. It's a grave error. The fast talking American style often only confirms another cultural member's preconceptions of American executives as shallow and self-serving.

Americans, here are a couple tips. Talk less, listen more. Try to connect on a personal level by finding common ground as a caring and compassionate person (do your homework—there are a number of socially appropriate topics for meaningful conversation in each culture) and watch for valuable non-verbal cues. Let others take the lead and suppress your American narcissistic (consider the possibility that individuals from other cultures can manage the task or challenge at least as well or yes, maybe even better than you) showboat tendency to take control. If you can't tolerate the silence as other slowly moving cultural players ponder how to react in a situation, then slowly and softly say something like, "Hmmmm... interesting... what do you think?" giving other players the green light to take the lead and set the pace.

It's really about evolving your cultural chameleon persona. Sometimes a take charge approach is needed and well received but quite often you are better served by taking a back seat. Trust your intuition and your ability to make the right call will evolve easier as your frequency of cross-cultural interaction increases.

Cultural Consideration 8

"She was demure, soft spoken and deferential. She used her charm and language abilities to build trust and close the deal with Japanese associates."

This seems like a natural lead-in to the cultural chameleon point I just noted. I have American friends who reacted to the above scenario by insinuating my Japanese friend was manipulative and inauthentic when projecting her Japanese persona. I disagree. She is multi-faceted and her personality is not one-dimensional. She simply put another aspect of her personality forward (in this case, her Japanese self) because her intuition told her it would be a good fit for her audience. She made a great decision. It was a brilliant, profitable and ethical move. We can be flexible, dynamic and intuitive in life and operate from a place of integrity.

Cultural Consideration 9

"Chinese and Taiwanese cultures have the same indirect communication style." I immediately sensed the entire group stiffen and disengage. Members of the group had misunderstood my analogy and thought I was inferring the Chinese and Taiwanese were the same people. Quickly I called a break and although I was aware of the political tensions between China and Taiwan, I didn't realize putting them under the same communication style umbrella would cause such havoc.

This is a good lesson for all of us to note when you have potentially warring groups under the same roof. In order not to offend, be particularly cautious and choose your words carefully. In this case, it was Chinese and Taiwanese. But this lesson could be applicable for a number of groups, cultural and non-cultural alike—from Democrats and Republicans to Christians and Muslims who may be housed in the same forum.

Cultural Considerations on the Flip Side

I think it's fair and important to ensure this book is not limited in approach by looking at a situation through one cultural lens and not considering another perspective.

For example, let's "flip" the following observations and considerations:

1. In the US, executives tend to be territorial in regard to their departments and take on a "mind your own business" reaction or "you take care of your department, I'll take care of mine" attitude if and/or when a peer questions them.

Could one argue that the American approach is superior by asserting American departmental leaders can more easily specialize in certain areas and thus, develop a level of expertise less easily obtained in German companies?

2. What, if any part of a hierarchical structure is valuable?

Could one argue the years of both life and professional experience are worthy of respect and seasoned opinions and contributions should be given priority and special consideration? Should groups who only have basic information regarding an organizational challenge defer to the older and seemingly wiser members of a group for a strategic response until the challenge facing the group becomes clearer?

3. What part, if any, of America's egalitarian value is potentially narrow-minded or lacking?

Could one argue equality-mindedness, while essential to avoiding judgment and maximizing participation, does not always foster awareness of limitations? Additionally, does equal mindedness discount the wisdom and insights of others who possess more knowledge or life experience? And finally, does equality foster an environment, which hinders the drive to cultivate skills or areas of expertise, by glossing over everyone and lumping people under one label?

4. Which parts, if any, of Germany's "slow methodical process" or America's "full speed ahead" is the most valuable approach and how does your opinion change, if at all, from small groups to large organizations?

These are interesting questions for you and your team to discuss and of course, many more cross cultural points to debate like:

- Are we evolved to the point where we can entertain the possibility that another culture's "flaw" may be the antidote to one of our cultural obstructions or setback?

- Would the incorporation of other cultural perspectives bring a greater sense of balance and position to America, resulting in future success?

This conversation goes both ways. For example, would a German corporation, firmly entrenched in a rigid operating mode, benefit from the looser American "go for it" approach and if so, how do you think changing the business norm and rules would be received by employees?

These questions are open to debate and don't necessarily have definitive right or wrong answers. Additionally, the reactions and/or potential solutions have to consider a number of variables, including company size, industry, target markets and so on.

In addition, I hope the outlined challenges and unique focus are thought provoking and left you wondering, as I do, if it is time for America to return to the drawing board, redefine the way we do business and weave other culture's successful approaches into our business mantra.

As you have probably surmised by now, the goal of all these final questions and the purpose of the book is to open our minds and expand our realm of possibilities beyond our own cultural limits. We can embrace the best the world has to offer, pragmatically identify what approaches meet our individual and organizational needs and then make Global Best Practices a reality. Together, we can maintain a strong and respectful presence in the global marketplace by becoming culturally savvy in thought, actions, behaviors, and mindset.

Acknowledgments

To J. Ruth Kelly, my amazing manager and social media assistant, whose guidance and diligence keeps me focused, my respect.

To Kristine Putt, my talented brand consultant who creates with vision and innovation, my admiration.

To Jenny Richards, my brilliant website master who has always stood by my side, my gratitude.

To all of you, my sincere thanks.